DATE DUE

The Exxon Valdez

Titles in the *American Disasters* series:

The Exxon Valdez
Tragic Oil Spill
ISBN 0-7660-1058-9

Hurricane Andrew
Nature's Rage
ISBN 0-7660-1057-0

The Oklahoma City Bombing
Terror in the Heartland
ISBN 0-7660-1061-9

Plains Outbreak Tornadoes
Killer Twisters
ISBN 0-7660-1059-7

San Francisco Earthquake, 1989
Death and Destruction
ISBN 0-7660-1060-0

The World Trade Center Bombing
Terror in the Towers
ISBN 0-7660-1056-2

The Exxon Valdez

Tragic Oil Spill

Victoria Sherrow

Enslow Publishers, Inc.

44 Fadem Road   PO Box 38
Box 699   Aldershot
Springfield, NJ 07081 Hants GU12 6BP
USA   UK

Library of Congress Cataloging-in-Publication Data

Sherrow, Victoria.
The Exxon Valdez: tragic oil spill / Victoria Sherrow.
    p. cm. — (American disasters)
  Includes bibliographical references (p.) and index.
  Summary: Details the grounding of the Exxon Valdez oil tanker in
Prince William Sound, discusses why this disaster happened, describes the
cleanup effort, and suggests lessons learned from the event.
  ISBN 0-7660-1058-9
  1. Oil spills—Environmental aspects—Alaska—Prince William Sound Region—
Juvenile literature. 2. Tankers—Accidents—Environmental
aspects—Alaska—Prince William Sound Region—Juvenile literature.
3. Exxon Valdez (Ship)—Juvenile literature. [1. Exxon Valdez (Ship)
2. Oil spills—Alaska—Prince William Sound Region. 3. Tankers—Accidents.]
I. Title II. Series.
TD427.P4S54 1998
363.738'2'097983—dc21   97-39182
                                      CIP
                                      AC

Printed in the United States of America.

10 9 8 7 6 5 4 3 2 1

Photo Credits: AP/Wide World Photos, pp. 1, 6, 9, 10, 17, 18, 22, 23, 25, 26,
27, 28, 30, 33, 34, 36, 37, 39, 40, 42.

Cover Photo: AP/Wide World Photos

Contents

CHAPTER 1

Ripped Apart!

It was a few minutes after midnight on March 24, 1989. The oil tanker *Exxon Valdez* was moving through Prince William Sound in Alaska.

Earlier that night, this supertanker had left the dock in Valdez (Val-DEEZ), Alaska. It had picked up 53 million gallons of North Slope crude oil from the trans-Alaska pipeline. Then, the fully loaded tanker had steamed south. It was set to move out of the sound, into the Pacific Ocean, until it reached Long Beach, California.

By midnight, the tanker had traveled twenty-eight miles from Valdez. It was no longer inside the usual shipping sea-lanes. Captain Joseph Hazelwood was not at the controls. Out on deck, the lookout saw that the ship was off course. A large reef stood less than one mile straight ahead.

Other crew members also spotted trouble. It was too late to change the course of this huge tanker, however. At 12:04 A.M., a booming noise rumbled throughout the ship. People on board heard scraping sounds as the reef tore into the hull. The ship groaned as it lurched to a stop.

Crew members were shocked to realize that they had slammed into Bligh Reef. The crash was so intense that several enormous boulders were jammed eight feet inside the tanker's steel hull. About six hundred feet of the hull had been ripped open.

Chief Mate James Kunkel hurried to the bridge. The ship was tilting sharply to one side. It might sink if it separated from the reef. The men would be plunged into frigid water and coated with oil. Kunkel later said, "I feared for my life."[1]

Sharp rocks had slashed eight cargo tanks. Crude oil poured from these holes. About two hundred thousand gallons a minute were streaming into Prince William Sound. Smelly fumes swirled around the ship.

The U.S. Coast Guard received radio messages from Captain Hazelwood. One message, recorded at 12:27 A.M. said, "We've fetched up hard aground north of Goose Island off Bligh Reef. And, uh, . . . evidently . . . leaking some oil, and . . . we're gonna be here for a while. . . ."[2] Captain Hazelwood and the crew then tried to move the ship safely off the rocks. At 2:00 A.M. they gave up and turned off the engines.

Soon, people throughout North America would hear about the *Exxon Valdez* oil spill. Some Alaskans had dreaded such an event for years. Their region is known for its beautiful beaches, spruce-covered mountains, and sparkling water. A vast number of plants and animals live there. It is called the Last Frontier.

The *Exxon Valdez* spill was clearly serious. Hours after

The picturesque village of Tatitlek, Alaska, is shown bordering Prince William Sound. The oil spill threatened to damage its beauty.

the collision, oil was still pouring from holes in the ship. Millions of gallons were floating across the water. Without quick, effective action, the millions of gallons left on board might also spill into Prince William Sound. This oil slick, pushed by tides and winds, would keep moving into other areas.

It was the worst oil spill that had ever occurred in North America, and it was caused by human error.

CHAPTER 2

A Disaster in the Making

The roots of the *Exxon Valdez* disaster date back to 1968. That year, large deposits of oil were found on Alaska's North Slope. Oil (petroleum) is a valued source of energy. It is often called black gold. The United States uses more oil than any other country in the world.

Many people were glad to hear about new sources of oil in the United States. Few nations have vast oil deposits. Most oil-rich countries are located in the Middle East. Some of those countries, such as Iran, have clashed with the United States. Their control over oil had enabled them to set high prices. Alaskan oil would make the United States less dependent on foreign imports.

Oil would also bring new jobs to Alaska. Thousands of people would be needed to set up wells and drill for oil. Others would work to build a pipeline for moving the oil to other parts of the state. The oil companies would need many employees for years to come.

The state of Alaska would earn hundreds of millions

of dollars by selling drilling rights to oil companies. These businesses would also pay high taxes to the state.

Plans were made to start drilling in Prudhoe Bay, on the Arctic coast. Scientists guessed there were billions of barrels of oil at this site. The oil companies planned to build a trans-Alaska pipeline. It would carry the oil from the wells at Prudhoe to ports in southern Alaska. From there, tankers loaded with crude would go to refineries in other states.

During the early 1970s, many Alaskans opposed the construction of the pipeline. Fishermen voiced strong concerns. They worried that an oil spill might occur. A spill could poison fish and damage the large fish hatcheries in their region. Other people pointed out the hazards to beaches, parks, and the wildlife on the Alaska coast.

Even so, in 1973 Congress approved the construction of the pipeline. Thousands of men and women worked to build it in harsh weather. Temperatures in this part of Alaska can sink to $-51°$ C ($-60°$ F). The finished pipeline was almost eight hundred miles long.

Ships began transporting oil four years later. By 1989, oil tankers were a familiar sight in Alaskan waters. About three tankers left Valdez, Alaska, every day.

Oil company officials continued to say that a serious spill was unlikely. If it occurred, emergency cleanup plans were in place.

Still, the disaster that was never supposed to have happened, did. The oil companies that were supposed to have responded were not prepared. They were stunned at the size of this spill. Nearly 11 million gallons of oil spilled. They lacked much of the equipment they needed for an efficient response.

As the cleanup began, investigators looked into the collision. The *Exxon Valdez*, built in 1986, had been in fine condition. The night of the crash had been clear with calm waters. The captain was well regarded and experienced. What could have gone wrong?

Investigators found out that the trip had begun quietly. Crew members said that Captain Hazelwood spent the first two hours in his cabin. At that time, a harbor pilot was in charge of guiding the ship.

The harbor pilot left, and Captain Hazelwood returned to the bridge. He warned the crew that icebergs were coming from Columbia Glacier. Hazelwood ordered them to change course to avoid the icebergs. He notified the U.S. Coast Guard about his movements.

Third Mate Gregory Cousins and seaman Robert Kagan were left at the controls. The captain told them to steer the tanker back to the regular traffic lane when they reached Busby Island. Hazelwood returned to his cabin at about seven minutes before midnight.

At this point, something went wrong. Third Mate Cousins gave an order to turn the tanker to the right. That should have started to bring the ship back into the correct lane. After a few more minutes, Cousins ordered a second turn. Yet the tanker was not where it should have been. Was something wrong with the steering equipment? Or had one of the men made a mistake?

Records taken from the ship's instruments told part of

the story. After the captain left the control room, the tanker moved in a straight line for eleven minutes. It shifted slightly to the right a few seconds before it hit Bligh Reef. The autopilot had accidentally been left on.

The spill was a ghastly blow to a region known for its natural beauty and clean environment. Prince William Sound is full of life, especially in the spring, when the spill occurred. Some of the birds that nest there are endangered. The forests and sea teem with plants and animals. Salmon hatch there. Fishermen also look forward to the herring run at that time of year.

The oil spill changed everything. Within hours, thousands of birds and sea otters died. News reports showed pictures of these pitiful small victims. Their feathers and fur were soaked with oil. People expressed anger and dismay as the slimy blackness spread across the sea.

To make matters worse, attempts to clean up the sound were faced with special problems. The waters there are cold. Warmer water would have helped the oil break down faster. Also, the shoreline is rocky and remote. The beaches contain a lot of gravel. Rocks and gravel provide a good place for oil to accumulate.

Faced with a huge task, response crews headed for Prince William Sound. Their goals were to keep more oil from spreading and to clean up as much as possible.

Meanwhile, shocked residents walked along the damaged beaches. Walter Meganack, Sr., said, "We walk our beaches, but instead of gathering life, we gather death. Dead birds. Dead otters. Dead seaweed."[1]

CHAPTER 3

A Desperate Fight

The morning after the spill brought sunshine and calm winds. Below beautiful skies, a deadly blackness made its way across the sea.

That first day, crews began to carefully unload the oil that remained on the *Exxon Valdez*. This was risky work. Seawater was put in the oil's place so the ship would stay balanced. The transfer had to be made without moving the ship too much. If the tanker had slipped off the rocks too fast, it might have sunk, spilling more oil.

The official plan for handling oil spills provided for a response within five hours. The Alyeska Pipeline Service Company was formed by the seven oil companies that own the pipeline. It is supposed to handle any problems that arise. Alyeska took twelve hours to reach the site.

The company was not prepared for a spill of this size. First, Alyeska spent hours gathering its equipment. It had to be found, loaded on barges, and then taken to the site of the spill.

Teams from the U.S. Coast Guard arrived to help contain and remove the oil. They brought skimmers— machines that pick up oil from the surface of the water. The oil is then pumped out of the area.

Some skimmers also work alone to suck up oil and transfer it into smaller ships.

Exxon pledged to clean up the spill. The company promised to "meet our obligations to all those who have suffered damage from the spill."[1] Their cleanup team had sixty skimmers. Twenty-two of these skimmers belonged to the U.S. Navy.

Volunteers from Russia, Norway, Denmark, and France also helped with the cleanup effort. Booms, plastic devices that float in the water, were used. They acted as a fence to prevent oil from spreading farther. Another type of boom moves oil toward a place where it can be removed more easily.

Booms were also set up to keep oil out of fisheries. Fishing is a major business in Prince William Sound. It brings in more than $100 million each year. The salmon industry alone was bringing in about $35 million each year before the spill. Hundreds of millions of young salmon swim upstream to Alaska salmon hatcheries each spring. Millions of freshly hatched salmon would die unless they were shielded from the spill. Other salmon spawn in streams that flow into Prince William Sound. Fishermen worried that oil would poison and kill these salmon. They also feared that oil would kill plankton. These are tiny plants and animals on which salmon feed.

Alaska state officials banned fishing in any areas the oil reached. They did not want contaminated fish to reach consumers. If people became sick after eating fish from Alaska, then the whole industry could be damaged.

These early efforts did not prevent the oil from moving across the sea and coastline. Within days, the oil had spread over hundreds of miles. People were complaining that the cleanup was slow and disorganized.

A Soviet skimmer works in the waters near Prince William Sound, hoping to contain the spread of oil.

*O*il cleanup workers prepare to vacuum the shoreline of Prince William Sound. Their rain gear is covered in oil residue.

Various private and public agencies were supposed to decide what to do if a spill occurred. The people who ran these agencies did not always agree. For example, they debated whether or not to use chemical dispersants. These are substances that act like detergents. They break down oil into smaller drops that mix more easily with water.

At first, the water was too calm for these chemicals to work. More tests were run. A federal official finally approved their use. By then, winds had reached speeds of

70 knots. Spraying chemical dispersants in heavy winds did little good. Even if the dispersants had worked, it would have taken many more gallons of them than Alaska had to disperse the oil spill. Years later, people were still wondering if these chemicals would have prevented some damage to the coastline.

Meanwhile, the damage continued both in the water and on land. Waves of oil washed ashore. Soon, a layer of sticky blackness clung to beaches and rocks.

The U.S. Coast Guard and federal and state agencies continued the cleanup effort. Local communities also took part.

Thousands of workers performed difficult, dirty jobs. Their clothing, shoes, and rain gear became coated with oil. They were surrounded by strong oil fumes, which caused breathing problems.

Despite a massive effort, the oil could not be controlled. Fast winds moved the slick along. Within a week, oil had moved to the Pacific Ocean.

Oil is made up of chemical compounds called hydrocarbons. They are mostly hydrogen and carbon. Some of the oil mixed with cold ocean water, forming a gummy oil-water combination called mousse (pronounced MOOSE). The mousse became so heavy that cleanup crews were unable to pump it out.

The slick also became more syrupy as the oil broke down. This occurred as a result of evaporation. Vapors rose into the air. They left behind a smelly, greasy substance.

It moved into channels and straits along the sound, leaving oil on the shoreline.

Helicopters, boats, and planes kept arriving at Prince William Sound. Thousands of people worked together to clean the soiled beaches. Some cleaning methods were as simple as wiping rocks by hand. Other people used more complex equipment. They aimed high-pressure water hoses at the oil. They tried to force it toward ships that would carry it away. People also used shovels, rakes, rags—even paper towels—to start cleaning the beach areas.

A method called bioremediation was also tried. Large amounts of fertilizer were dumped on some oily shores. This fertilizer increased the growth and activity of bacteria that "eat" oil, turning it into less harmful substances. Despite some success, very little oil was actually removed this way.

In total, some eleven thousand people worked to fight the effects of the spill. Exxon hired fishermen and others who had been deprived of their regular jobs as a result of the spill.

One of the saddest jobs was removing the bodies of dead animals. Kelsey Crago, a fisherman, said,

> We've picked up about 3,000 birds in the last five days. Most of them were murres, killed around the Barren Islands northeast of here. They keep drifting in with the tide. We're collecting the bodies to keep the bears and eagles from eating them.[2]

Animals and plants living in the sound were tragic victims of the spill. While some workers cleaned up the mess, others tried to rescue birds and other animals.

CHAPTER 4

Struggling to Survive

At the time of the spill, Prince William Sound was home to millions of living creatures. One of North America's largest sea otter populations made its home there. Scientists guess there had been about ten thousand otters.[1]

Some four hundred thousand birds also lived in Prince William Sound year-round. Another million arrived each spring.[2] There were also about 10 million shorebirds and waterfowl. Among them were loons and large numbers of marbled murrelets.

Other animals inhabited wooded areas near the shores. Deer, river otters, bears, and bald eagles were numerous. When the spill hit, many animals had just awakened from a long winter's rest. Others were returning to the sound after wintering in warmer places.

Heartbreaking sights surrounded the cleanup crews. Oil-soaked dead or dying birds lay on the oily shores. Dead sea otters were swept in with the tides. Seal pups called

A large bird population lived on Prince William Sound before the tragic oil spill. Time will tell what the long-range effects on the many different bird species will be.

for their dead mothers. The animals must have suffered terribly as oil soaked their eyes, ears, and skin.

By August thousands of dead birds had been found. Many other dead birds and animals sank to the bottom of the sea and were never found. In all, some thirty thousand birds died from the spill.[3] Some died from the cold after oil matted their feathers. Others were poisoned by eating oiled food. Still other birds drowned. Covered with oil, they could no longer float or fly. Among the casualties were 150 bald eagles.[4]

Of the marine mammals, the otters were hardest hit. At least twenty-eight hundred sea otters died.[5] Oil poisoned many of them. Others died from hypothermia. Hypothermia results when the body temperature stays too low for too long. After oil drenched the otters' fur, they could not stay warm. Their fur could no longer

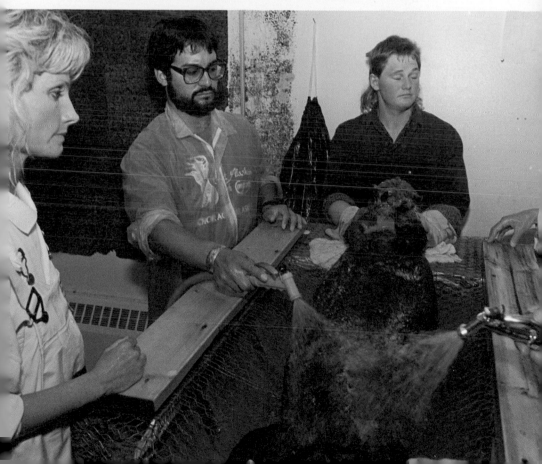

A rescued otter is restrained and washed by workers at a local animal hospital. Rescuers have been busy capturing and cleaning oil slicked animals.

protect them from the cold air and water temperatures. Animals that were still alive were taken to rescue centers. Veterinarians, assistants, and volunteers worked to save animals' lives. Workers came from many countries to help these creatures.

At the Valdez Sea Otter Rescue Center, twenty-four people worked day and night. They struggled to save lives and ease suffering. Many of the otters brought to the center had weak heartbeats and could hardly breathe. They were in a state of shock.

Workers carefully washed the oil off their fur with liquid detergent. Then the otters were soaked in warm baths. They were given injections of charcoal solution inside their stomachs to fight the poisonous effects of the oil. It took an entire day to clean each otter. Half of the 156 otters that arrived at this center survived.[6]

In the summer after the spill, 348 otters were treated at rescue centers, but most died after they were released. The cost of this effort was about $28 million.[7]

Birds received painstaking care, too. Many were so scared they received tranquilizers—medication to calm them. Workers used toothbrushes to massage soapsuds into their feathers. They had to be very gentle to avoid damaging these delicate parts. The soap was then rinsed out completely to prevent skin rashes.

The birds needed rest to recover. Some would not eat. Workers fed them by hand. They massaged the birds' throats to get the food down.

Seals also suffered from poisonous effects. About

An oil-soaked bird gets a gentle massage with a toothbrush and soapsuds.

three hundred harbor seals died.[8] Oil polluted their skin and hair. It moved inside their bodies and damaged their organs. As female seals died, they could not feed their pups. Many orphaned pups soon died, too. Some orphans were taken to rehabilitation centers. The total number of dead seals may never be known. One biologist said, "Seals sink when they die, and that's why they are hard to find."[9]

Whales seemed to survive the effects of the oil better than some of the other animals. Their blubber kept them warm even when oil coated their bodies. However, thirteen killer whales did die from the spill.

Oil in the water hurt many animals' food supply. It reached plankton and various plants. Smaller fish eat these plants. In turn, sea mammals eat the fish. Animals of all kinds were affected by oil in the food supply. These effects cannot all be determined.

A village of Alaska Aleut (natives) was located about six miles from Bligh Reef. For centuries, the Aleuts had

This California gray whale is among the casualties of the *Exxon Valdez* oil spill.

Oil washes ashore as volunteers do their best to clean it, by soaking it up with rags.

hunted and fished for food. They feared the oil would destroy the birds, fish, and mammals they ate. They waited anxiously for the results of lab tests on birds and other animals. These tests would show whether the animals were safe to eat. Their entire way of life was at stake.

One of their main foods was shellfish. Shellfish lack effective ways to remove oil from their systems. Violet Yeston, a member of a village in Port Graham, was concerned. She said, "People are afraid of eating a lot of shellfish. We eat them at our own risk. . . . It's very disturbing, the disruption it's caused in our community."[10]

As people worried about the future, the oil continued to spread and change. More oil mousse coated the sound. Tar balls made of oil and plants littered the shores. The most powerful skimmers could not suck up the thick oil.

On shore, oil sank under the rocks and into the ground. Tides redeposited oil on beaches that had just been "cleaned." In June, scientist Bruce Goldstein walked along the sound with a biologist. Goldstein commented, "Exxon would need a miracle to clean this beach and all

Colored tarps mark the spots where oil still washes up onto the rocks. Tides that continually carry the spilled oil ashore make permanent cleanup difficult.

the others by winter." The biologist replied, "You know, we're standing on a cleaned beach."[11]

In time, the oil traveled six hundred miles southwest of the original spill. It seeped into a national forest, three national parks, and five state parks. It also tainted four state critical habitat areas, four national wildlife refuges, and a state game sanctuary.

On June 23, the *Exxon Valdez* tanker was towed from the crash site to a nearby island. The hull was fixed, and the tanker left for California. There it would be completely repaired.

The tanker left behind destruction and many questions. In the wake of this disaster, lawsuits would be filed. New regulations and laws would be made. Nobody wanted another spill like this one.

Harsh Lessons

After the *Exxon Valdez* disaster, people demanded stricter laws to prevent oil spills. They demanded that Exxon be held accountable. They insisted on better cleanup methods if any spills occurred again. They complained that this cleanup had been ineffective.

One year after the spill, Exxon and the government studied the Alaskan shoreline. The cleanup was far from finished. A sticky residue of oil continued to form as time passed. Workers were still cleaning up in 1997, eight years after the spill.

A survey done in 1992 showed patches of oil still on the surface of some shoreline. Subsurface oil remained, too. Prince William Sound and the Kenai Peninsula had the most remaining oil.

In some places, oil still polluted shellfish beds more than five years after the spill. Dave Cobb was the manager of the Valdez Hatchery in 1994. He told a reporter for *USA Today*, "Those beaches are supposed to be clean but all you have to do to find oil is turn over a few rocks. It's down there."[1]

Fishermen had ongoing problems. The 1989 herring season was lost. The Pacific herring run in the sound collapsed in 1994. That spring, the number of herring returning to spawn was the lowest ever observed. In the mid-1990s, herring fisheries were shut down. The herring had spots on them. People feared they had been damaged by the oil spill.

There was a large salmon catch in 1990, possibly because their normal predators were killed by the oil spill. However, the salmon runs declined greatly after 1992. Scientists have found genetic damage in the sound's pink salmon population.

Fishermen blamed poor catches on the lasting effects of the oil. Rick Ott spoke for the United Fishermen of Alaska. He said that the spill had hurt his community "in its pocket and in its soul."[2] Henry Rosing, a fisherman from Whitier, spoke with reporter Noah Adams. Rosing said that his fishing business had once netted from $40,000 to $50,000 each year. But, said Rosing, "After the spill I have not made any money. I've made no net. I've taken two years of loss."[3]

The Alaskan native communities continued to suffer. Fish and seal populations were lower. Hunters had to travel farther to find food. People were afraid to eat mussels. Seabirds that eat mussels were not recovering their normal populations, either.

In the summer of 1994, the federal government tried

*T*hese sea lions play in the water and on the rocks of Prince William Sound. They all have some oil on them.

a new method to clean beds of mussels. It sponsored a project to replace thirty-eight tons of oily sediment with clean sediment.

There were some hopeful signs. People had feared oil would sink to the bottom of the sound. This can happen when drops of oil mix with sand. Although studies revealed a good deal of oil, it was not as bad as many had feared.

Scientists at the Alaska Division of Environmental Health also had good news. The head of the laboratory announced that they had tested five thousand fish sent in by state inspectors and native fishermen. He said, "So far we have found no crude-oil contamination."[4]

People picket a New Jersey Exxon station, calling for a statewide boycott of the company, following the *Exxon Valdez* oil spill.

By 1996, bald eagles had recovered to normal numbers. Studies showed no difference in the numbers that were living in oiled versus nonoiled areas.[5]

> Exxon budgeted $20 million to study the spill for one year. The company's science adviser was Al Maki. He said, We've selected more than 300 people with the best credentials in the country to do an accurate, science-based assessment of the spill. We now have thousands of water and sediment samples from Prince William Sound through Kodiak and the Alaska Peninsula.[6]

Many local residents and scientists were angered by Exxon's well-funded public relations campaign to try to convince the world that not much damage was caused by the spill.

Scientists continued to monitor wildlife. The sea otter population recovered somewhat by 1991. Other animals did not fare as well. As of 1995, Pacific herring had still not recovered. Their numbers were far lower than they had been before the oil spill. Some scientists admit the sound may never fully recover.

Bird populations were also studied. The murre population was slowly recovering. Fewer chicks were born in the years after the spill, however. Scientists guessed that it would take between twenty and seventy years for a complete recovery.[7] Harlequin ducks in the oiled areas were not producing as many young as normal.

As scientists studied the spill, citizens continued to express their outrage. The National Transportation Safety Board (NTSB) issued a report on the probable causes of the collision. According to the report, the third mate had not properly guided the tanker because of fatigue and excessive workload. The captain failed "to provide a proper navigation watch because of impairment from alcohol," said the board. Exxon Corporation failed "to provide a fit master and a rested and sufficient crew" for the tanker. The NTSB also said Exxon had not given its personnel enough training.[8]

The Exxon Corporation also faced several lawsuits. In

Workers spray pressurized water on the beach at Prince William Sound. The oil spill was caused by an alcohol-impaired captain.

C aptain of the *Exxon Valdez*, Joseph Hazelwood (left), was sentenced to 1,000 hours of community service— cleaning the beaches in Prince William Sound.

1989, the state of Alaska filed a multibillion dollar lawsuit against the company. The federal government filed a criminal lawsuit against Exxon. The company was charged with dumping oil, polluting the water, and harming wildlife.

In 1990, Captain Hazelwood was convicted of the negligent discharge of oil. He was sentenced to one thousand hours of community service cleaning beaches in Prince William Sound.

A year later, Exxon agreed to pay $900 million over a period of ten years. Part of this money would repay state and federal governments the costs they had to pay as a result of the oil spill. These governments could also claim up to $100 million for restoring resources in the future. The first payment was made in December 1991.

Exxon was also fined $150 million. This fine was the largest ever set for a crime against the environment. The company had already spent $2.1 billion cleaning up the spill. They had also paid some claims made by private citizens. As a result, the court said they need pay only $25 million of the $150 million fine.

Of that, $12 million was sent to the North American Wetlands Conservation Fund; $13 million went to the Victims of Crime Fund.

The *Exxon Valdez* Oil Spill Trustee Council was also formed under this agreement. The council includes three state and three federal trustees. They have supervised the restoration process. Habitat protection is a big part of this plan. Large new parcels of land were purchased and protected for fish, birds, and other animals.

The council also sponsors education programs. One of these programs is the Youth Area Watch. Beginning in 1995, students from the Chugach school district worked alongside research scientists. They examined different parts of the environment that were affected by the spill. Students gathered information and studied samples in the lab as part of this hands-on learning experience.

In 1994, a federal jury in Anchorage found Exxon guilty of recklessness. Reporter Peter Kenyon said, "A cheer went up in the courtroom as the verdict was read. . . ."[9] This verdict permitted more civil lawsuits against Exxon.

*A*laska governor Walter Hickel tells reporters in Washington of Exxon's agreement to pay $900 million to complete all cleanup from the oil spill.

A group made up of fishermen, native hunters, and others sued the company.

A jury awarded the group $5 billion. This money was to be divided among the 14,000 plaintiffs (people who brought the suit). It was the second-largest jury award ever in the United States. Exxon appealed the judgment. As of 1997, Exxon had not paid any money to these parties.

Jim O'Brien was a retired Coast Guard officer who headed one of Exxon's cleanup teams. He said, "There's an important thing people must realize in planning for a spill this size: No amount of equipment will clean it all up, even if they give you a month's notice to get ready."[10]

O'Brien pointed out the problems of working in a large

A worker skims the oil off the waters of Prince William Sound. Better planning might have made a difference in the extent of this disaster.

area of water. It takes time to send out the boats, skimmers, and support vessels that are needed. He said, "Skimmers need barges to collect their oil. Crews need food, ships need fuel, and somebody has to collect the garbage. And nothing works if the weather's bad."[11]

Prevention is the best tactic. Laws and regulations have been passed to prevent future spills or at least limit the damage. In 1990, Congress passed the Oil Pollution Act. A company cannot ship oil into the United States until it presents a plan to prevent spills. It must have a detailed containment and cleanup plan in case of an emergency. Oil tankers are now more strictly inspected. Their operation is also more closely controlled than it was in 1989. Crew members are required to have more training.

Inspections and technology also aim to prevent spills. Special X-ray machines can detect cracks inside oil pipelines. When spills occur at sea, laboratories can do tests to pinpoint which ship was carrying the oil. Government officials check ships and storage tanks to make sure they are sound.

The oil companies funded the development of more efficient response centers located along the coastline. These centers were given enough equipment and trained staff to deal with a large spill (about 8.4 million gallons). After tankers leave the pipeline terminal, two escort vessels accompany them to Hinchinbrook. The tankers carry a boom, skimmers, and a workboat.

Human error causes the majority of oil spills. People may fall asleep on the job or abuse drugs or alcohol. Bad weather conditions have led to other accidents. Persons who may have to pilot a ship through Prince William Sound are tested for alcohol as they leave the pipeline terminal. As of 1994, about 25 percent of the world's oil tankers had double hulls, sides, or bottoms. New and better ways to clean up oil have been studied, too.

Laws require people to notify the Coast Guard if a gallon or more of oil spills into the water. People are not allowed to hide such a spill or use their own chemicals to

Workers try to clean the rocks on the shores of Prince William Sound. Human error caused this tragic oil spill. Many safeguards have been carried out since then.

try to clean it up. They may be fined or sued for damaging the environment.

Still, money cannot replace what an oil spill takes away. How can a dollar value be placed on unspoiled natural beauty or on the lives of thousands of birds, plants, and animals? Mary Kompkoff of Chenega Bay says,

> No money in the world will change what Exxon did to us. No money in the world will ever make it the same.[12]

Other Major Oil Spills

NAME	PLACE	DATE	CAUSE
Pipeline	West Delta, Louisiana	October 15, 1967	Dragging anchor
OIL SPILLED 6,720,000 gallons			
Torrey Canyon	Cornwall, England	1967	Grounding
OIL SPILLED 35,000,000 gallons			
World Glory	Off South Africa	June 13, 1968	Hull failure
OIL SPILLED 13,524,000 gallons			
Storage tank	Sewaren, New Jersey	November 4, 1969	Tank rupture
OIL SPILLED 8,400,000 gallons			
Keo	Off Massachusetts	November 5, 1969	Hull failure
OIL SPILLED 8,820,000 gallons			
Tanker	Off Japan	November 30, 1971	Ship broke in half
OIL SPILLED 6,258,000 gallons			
Argo Merchant	Nantucket, Massachusetts	December 15, 1976	Grounding
OIL SPILLED 7,700,000 gallons			
Ekofisk oil field	North Sea	April 22, 1977	Well blowout
OIL SPILLED 8,200,000 gallons			
Hawaiian Patriot	Northern Pacific	1977	Caught fire
OIL SPILLED 29,000,000 gallons			
Amoco Cadiz	English Channel off coast of Brittany, France	March 16, 1978	Grounding
OIL SPILLED 65,000,000 to 68,000,00 gallons			
Burmah Agate	Galveston Bay, Texas	November 1, 1979	Collision
OIL SPILLED 10,700,000 gallons			

Chapter 1. Ripped Apart!

1. Bryan Hodgson, "Alaska's Big Spill: Can the Wilderness Heal?" *National Geographic*, January 1990, p. 32.

2. Ibid.

Chapter 2. A Disaster in the Making

1. "Lingering Concerns Over the *Exxon Valdez* Spill," National Public Radio *(Earth Explorer)* program, February 1, 1995.

Chapter 3. A Desperate Fight

1. David Foster, "What Price Pollution?" *Los Angeles Times*, July 24, 1994, p. A-1.

2. Bryan Hodgson, "Alaska's Big Spill: Can the Wilderness Heal?" *National Geographic*, January 1990, p. 28.

Chapter 4. Struggling to Survive

1. Douglas B. Lee, "Tragedy in Alaska Waters," *National Geographic*, August 1989, p. 262.

2. Ibid.

3. R. Hartung, "Assessment of the Potential for Long-Term Toxicological Effects of the *Exxon Valdez* Oil Spill on Birds and Mammals," in American Society for Testing and Materials (ASTM), *Exxon Valdez Oil Spill: Fate and Effects in Alaskan Waters* (Philadelphia: ASTM, 1996), pp. 693–725.

4. Bryan Hodgson, "Alaska's Big Spill: Can the Wilderness Heal?" *National Geographic*, January 1990, p. 8.

5. Statistic from Oil Spill Public Information Center (OSPIC) at <http://www.alaska.net/~ospic.>

6. Hartung, pp. 702–704; Hodgson, p. 29.

7. Terry Carr, *Spill! The Story of the Exxon Valdez* (New York: Franklin Watts, 1991), p. 47.

8. American Fisheries Society, Proceedings of the *Exxon Valdez* Oil Spill Symposium, 1996, quoted in Oil Spill Public Information Center (OSPIC) website.

9. Quoted in Hodgson, p. 25.

10. Beth Tornes, "The Sound Is Still Not Clean: The Impact of the *Exxon Valdez* Oil Spill on the Native People of Prince William Sound," *News From Indian Country*, September 15, 1995, pp. P.G.

11. Bruce Goldstein, "The Folly of the *Exxon Valdez* Cleanup," *Earth Island Journal*, January 1, 1991, p. 30.

Chapter 5. Harsh Lessons

1. Rae Tyson, "Valdez Cleanup Is Skin-Deep," *Newsweek* March 22, 1994, p. 3.

2. Ibid., p. 3.

3. "Alaskan Fishermen Win Award in Exxon Oil Spill," National Public Radio, *Morning Edition*, August 12, 1994.

4. Bryan Hodgson, "Alaska's Big Spill: Can the Wilderness Heal?" *National Geographic*, January 1990, p. 16.

5. P.G. Wells, J.N. Butler, and J.S. Hughes, "Introduction, Overview, and Issues," in *American Society for Testing and Materials, Exxon Valdez Oil Spill: Fate and Effects in Alaskan Waters* (Philadelphia: ASTM, 1996), pp. 3–38.

6. Hodgson, p. 20.

7. J.A. Wiens, "Recovery of Seabirds Following the *Exxon Valdez* Oil Spill," in American Society for Testing and Materials (ASTM), *Exxon Valdez Oil Spill: Fate and Effects in Alaskan Waters* (Philadelphia: ASTM, 1996), pp. 854–893.

8. National Transportation Safety Board Marine Accident Report, 1990.

9. "Alaska Jury Finds Exxon Acted Recklessly," National Public Radio, *All Things Considered*, June 13, 1994.

10. Hodgson, p. 39.

11. Ibid.

12. David Foster, "What Price Pollution?" *Los Angeles Times*, July 24, 1994, p. A-1.

bacteria—Tiny living cells that can only be viewed through a microscope.

bioremediation—Methods that use naturally occurring processes to remedy a problem. (For example, applying fertilizer to oil so that the bacteria will turn the oil into less harmful substances.)

blubber—Layers of fat under the skin of a whale that help keep the whale warm in cold water.

boom—A device placed around an oil slick to act as a fence to keep the oil in.

crude—Oil from the ground that has not yet been refined for use.

dispersant—A substance that acts in the same way as a detergent to break down oil into smaller drops.

evaporate—To turn into vapor from a solid or liquid form.

hull—The sides and bottom of a ship.

hydrocarbon—Chemical compounds that are made up of hydrogen and carbon molecules.

mousse—A gummy combination of oil and water.

oil slick—A circular layer of spilled oil.

plankton—Very small plants and animals that float in seas and lakes. Larger sea creatures eat plankton.

skimmer—A device used to remove oil from the surface of water.

Anderson, Madelyn Klein. *Oil Spills*. New York: Franklin Watts, 1990.

Brown, Joseph E. *Oil Spills: Danger in the Sea*. New York: Dodd, Mead, 1978.

Carr, Terry. *Spill: The Story of the Exxon Valdez*. New York: Franklin Watts, 1991.

Keller, David. *Great Disasters: The Most Shocking Moments in History*. New York: Avon Books, 1990.

Schouweiler, Tom. *The Exxon Valdez Oil Spill*. San Diego, Calif.: Lucent Books, 1991.

Stephen, R.J. *Oil Rigs*. New York: Franklin Watts, 1986.

Stefoff, Rebecca. *Environmental Disasters*. New York: Chelsea House Publishers, 1994.

Internet

Oil Spill Public Information Center

<http://www.alaska.net/~ospic>

Official Exxon Valdez Oil Spill Restoration Site

<http://www.oilspill.state.ak.us>